Why did pirates bury treasure?

Miles Kelly

First published as Why Why Why in 2005 by
Miles Kelly Publishing Ltd, Bardfield Centre,
Great Bardfield, Essex, CM7 4SL, UK

This edition published 2010

2 4 6 8 10 9 7 5 3 1

Editorial Director Belinda Gallagher
Art Director Jo Brewer
Editorial Assistant Amanda Askew
Author Catherine Chambers
Volume Designer Sophie Pelham
Cover Designer Jo Brewer
Indexer Helen Snaith
Production Manager Elizabeth Brunwin
Reprographics Anthony Cambray, Ian Paulyn
Assets Manager Bethan Ellish
Cover Artist Mike White
Character Cartoonist Mike Foster

All artwork from the Miles Kelly Archives

ISBN 978-1-84810-220-0

Printed in China

British Library Cataloguing-in-Publication Data
A catalogue record for this book is available
from the British Library

Made with paper from a sustainable forest

www.mileskelly.net
info@mileskelly.net

www.factsforprojects.com
The one-stop homework helper –
pictures, facts, videos, projects and more

Contents

What is a pirate?

A pirate attack

Pirates are people who steal from ships and ports. As soon as the first ships began to carry goods, pirates began to attack them. About 600 years ago, there were many pirates sailing on the seas and oceans around the world.

Hairy pirates!

'Barbarossa' was a nickname for two pirate brothers. 'Barbarossa' means 'Redbeard' — because they both had red beards!

Who was afraid of the Barbarossas?

Every sailor was afraid of the two Barbarossa brothers! They were pirates who attacked ships about 500 years ago. One of the brothers captured the town of Algiers in North Africa. The other attacked ships that belonged to the Pope, who was the leader of the Christian church.

Make

Make your own Barbarossa mask. Draw your pirate's face on card. Use red wool to make a big red beard.

Did all pirates want treasure?

Pirates from the Mediterranean were called corsairs. They didn't want treasure. Instead, they took people from ships and ports and sold them as slaves. Corsairs also captured rich people. They were paid a lot of money to release them.

Corsairs and their ships

Who stole the Spanish gold?

About 500 years ago, Spanish captains sailed to the Americas. There they found gold, silver and jewels. The Spanish stole it from the American people and took it back to Spain. Pirates often attacked the Spanish ships before they got home and took the treasure from them.

Spanish captains and their treasure

Act

Try to act out your own story about Spanish and English captains. One is trying to steal treasure from the other.

When were pirates not pirates?

English captains such as John Hawkins raided Spanish treasure ships. England and Spain were enemies at this time, so the English thought it was okay to steal from the Spanish. The captains wanted to be called 'privateers' instead of 'pirates'.

Pirate queen!

Queen Elizabeth I of England encouraged her sea captains to be privateers. However, the privateers were often robbed before they reached England!

Can you be a pirate with one leg?

Francois Le Clerc

Yes! Francois Le Clerc was a dangerous pirate with just one leg. In the 1550s, he raided Caribbean islands owned by Spain. He captured the port of Havana on the island of Cuba. No one would pay Le Clerc to give up the port, so he burned it to the ground.

Were 'sea dogs' really dogs?

Some famous captains were called 'sea dogs'. They were clever and daring. Francis Drake was the most famous sea dog. In 1572 he attacked the Spanish in Central America and stole lots of silver.

The Spanish being attacked by Drake

What was the best weapon?

On the Caribbean island of Hispaniola, men hunted wild pigs and cooked them on open fires. They used a special knife to cut the pigs up. Later, the knife blade was made into a short, wide sword. It was called a cutlass. Pirates and other sailors began to fight with it.

What a treasure!

Francis Drake once attacked a treasure store. But when he broke open the store, it was empty!

Who were the buccaneers?

Buccaneers were daring pirates who sailed on the Caribbean Sea. They stole treasure from Spanish and English ships. The first buccaneers were criminals and wanderers. They lived on the island of Hispaniola.

Buccaneers

Design

Design your own pirate sword. Cut your sword out of card. You could draw patterns on it and decorate it with 'stolen' jewels.

Did sailors fight the pirates?

Sailors fought hard against pirates when they were attacked.
But they didn't try to fight Francis L'Ollonais in the 1660s. He was very cruel and tortured his prisoners. When Francis attacked a ship, the captain and sailors usually gave up without a fight.

Captain surrendering

What did pirates do with their money?

Pirates sold their treasure to people at the docks. They usually made lots of money. Most of the money was spent in public houses!

Spend! Spend! Spend!

Pirates could spent 3000 pieces of silver in one night. That's about ₤45,000 in today's money!

Francis L'Ollonais

Where was there a pirate paradise?

Port Royal was a harbour on the island of Jamaica. A strong fort guarded the harbour. Pirates could even mend their ships in the docks. Jamaica was ruled by the English, who left the pirates alone.

Paint

Paint a pirate scene with ships and a port. There might be lots of ships, with the pirates carrying their treasure onto dry land.

Pirates in Port Royal

Did pirates move about?

Yes, they did. Pirates in the Caribbean heard about great treasures to be found in the Indian Ocean. So many moved to Madagascar, an island off the coast of Africa. This island was a good place for pirates to hide as it was covered in forest.

Pirates on Madagascar →

Attack!

In the 1700s, an African pirate called Kanhoji Angria attacked the British from his forts along India's coast.

Pirate attack on a treasure ship

Did the Indian Ocean get crowded?

Pirates from many countries sailed on the Indian Ocean. Over 500 years ago, Portuguese pirates sailed from Africa to India. From there they went on to the South China Seas. On the way they stole silks, spices, jewels and gold.

Who was top pirate?

In the 1690s, Henry Avery was known as 'The Arch Pirate'. He was the top pirate of his time. Henry attacked an Indian emperor's treasure ship. The women on board were so frightened that they jumped into the sea.

Find

Look at a map of the world and try to find India, Africa and Portugal. Can you find the Indian Ocean and Caribbean Sea, too?

Could women be pirates?

Yes, they could! Mary Read dressed up as a man and became a sailor in the 1700s. Her ship was raided by pirates and Mary decided to join them. Her ship was raided by 'Calico Jack' and his wife, Anne Bonney. Mary made friends with Anne and they fought against the navy.

Mary Read and Anne Bonney

Make

Make a plate of food for a pirate's prisoner! Take a paper plate and stick on cut-out food – such as caterpillars!

Whose prisoners ate caterpillars?

Ching Shih was a Chinese pirate. In 1807, she controlled many ships that raided China's coast. Ching Shih was a great leader. She had very strict rules for her sailors. Her prisoners had to eat caterpillars in boiled rice!

Ching Shih

Baldy!

Grace O'Malley shaved her head to look more like her sailors. She was given the nickname 'Baldy'!

Who said she was sorry?

Grace O'Malley went to sea when she was a young girl. She ended up controlling pirate ships off the coast of Ireland. Grace had 20 ships under her command. In 1593 Grace asked Queen Elizabeth I of England to forgive her for being a pirate.

What were the best ships?

A galley ship

Stern (back)

Oars

Water and stores (middle)

Pirate ships had to be very fast! Many were small and easy to sail. Schooners were ships that had two masts. Corsairs sailed in galleys — ships that had oars as well as sails. The captain had a cabin in the stern (back of the ship). Treasure, gunpowder and food were stored in the hold, beneath the deck.

Where did pirates sleep?

Most pirates slept on the deck unless the weather was bad. Some put up hammocks below deck in the middle of the ship. It was cramped, smelly and noisy. This made some pirates ill. So did their food. They didn't eat enough fruit and vegetables!

Recycling!

Pirates even stole their prisoners' clothes! They usually sold them, but sometimes kept the best items for themselves.

Sails

Write

Look at the picture of the galley. Write a guided tour of the ship. Describe how the pirates lived on it, too.

Bow (front)

What did pirates eat?

Pirates mostly ate dry biscuits and pickled meat when on board ship. They hunted for fresh meat when they landed on islands. They also collected fresh water and fruit. Pirate cooks often had only one arm or leg. They couldn't fight, so they cooked!

Who was afraid of a flag?

Merchant seamen were terrified when they saw the flag of a pirate ship. Early flags were bright red. By the 1700s, pirates flew black flags. Each pirate captain added his or her own symbol. Sometimes this was the famous white skull-and-crossbones.

Were buccaneers heroes?

Buccaneers were violent thieves. Some people thought they were heroes. Bartholomew Roberts was a buccaneer. His nickname was Black Bart. He was handsome and bold, yet he never drank anything stronger than tea! In the 1720s, he captured 400 ships.

Pirate flag

Duck!

When pirates attacked a ship, they shot at sailors working on the sails. They also shot at the helm, the steering area of the ship.

Where was the treasure?

Sailors often hid their treasure. Pirates had to break down walls and doors to find it. They threatened their prisoners until they revealed the treasure. Pirates had frightening weapons such as knives, daggers and pistols.

Pirates looking for treasure

Design

Design your own pirate flag. Choose a bold colour. You could draw your own frightening symbol on it.

What was the best treasure?

Gold and silver was the best pirate treasure. It could be gold or silver coins, plain bars or made into fine ornaments. Silk cloth and hardwoods such as ebony were also valuable. So was ivory. But pirates were not so happy with cotton, coal or iron.

Pirates and their stolen treasure

Spicy sands!

Spices from India and Sri Lanka were very valuable, but they were difficult to sell. Pirates often dumped them overboard. These spices piled up on the beaches.

Was the treasure shared?

The captain was in charge of sharing out the treasure. Officers got more than ordinary sailors. The cook and the carpenter got less because they didn't fight. Captains tried to divide everything fairly. Unhappy pirates might attack the captain and take over the ship!

Make

Make a mini treasure chest. Take a small box and paint it to look like wood. Then fill it with painted cut-out jewels.

Where were all the jewels?

Pirates stole jewels from ships all over the world. Diamonds came from Africa. Red rubies and blue sapphires came from Burma. Green emeralds were mined in Colombia. Divers scooped up shiny pearls from the Persian Gulf.

Treasure chest

Why did pirates bury treasure?

Pirates are believed to have buried treasure in secret places so that no-one else could steal it. Captain William Kidd was a famous pirate who was arrested in 1699. After he was captured he claimed that he had buried treasure worth £100,000!

Captain William Kidd

Marooned pirate

What was marooning?

If a pirate broke his captain's rules, he could be marooned. This meant that the pirate was left alone on a deserted island. He was given a few things such as a gun and some water, while his shipmates sailed away without him.

Was the captain safe?

Sometimes sailors hated their captain. They took over the ship and got rid of the captain. This was called a mutiny. Captain Jeremy Randall's crew mutinied against him in 1684. He was left on an island with three men, a gun, a canoe and a turtle net.

Pirates burying treasure

Guess

Draw a treasure island map. Stick numbered flaps on it. Under one flap lies the treasure. Your friends must guess which one it is.

No rules!

There was no code of rules between one pirate ship and another. So pirates happily attacked other pirates and stole their treasure!

What were pirates scared of?

Shipwreck was a pirate's greatest fear. Terrible storms could blow up in the warm waters around the Caribbean, the Indian Ocean and the Far East. In 1712, a storm blasted Port Royal in Jamaica. Winds smashed ships to pieces.

Shipwreck

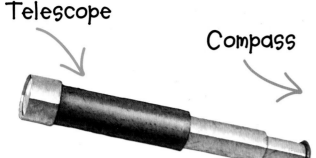
Telescope

Compass

Map

How did pirates find their way?

Pirates used the position of the Sun and stars to guide them in the right direction. They also used a compass to help them. A telescope helped pirates to see landmarks and work out their position. Pirates used maps to find their way on land.

Write

Pretend you are captain of a pirate ship. Write down all the jobs that are carried out on board every day.

Round and round!

Captain William Dampier was a brilliant navigator. This means he knew where he was going! In the 1680s he sailed around the world three times.

How did pirates save a sinking ship?

Pirates tried to pump out water if the ship was leaking. Sometimes ships 'ran aground'. This means they got stuck in shallow water. The pirates had to throw out anything heavy. This helped the ship to refloat. Sometimes they threw out food barrels and cannons.

What happened to Blackbeard?

Blackbeard was one of the most famous pirates. His real name was Edward Teach. He put ribbons in his black beard and stuck lit matches under his hat! In 1718, an officer called Robert Maynard killed Blackbeard.

Robert Maynard   Blackbeard

Sea of boats!

Ching-Chi-Ling was a famous Chinese pirate leader. He had more than 1000 boats, called junks.

Who was guilty?

Captured pirates ended up in court. Judges decided that most sailors on pirate ships were guilty. A sailor who carried a gun or fired a cannon was found guilty. So were people who just carried stolen goods.

Draw

Draw a picture of your own very fierce pirate. You can stick things on the picture – like Blackbeard's matchsticks under his hat!

Were pirates punished?

There was often a reward for catching pirates – dead or alive. Many pirates ended up in prison. Most died there. One of the worst prisons was Newgate in London. It was filthy, smelly and cramped. Most pirates starved or died of disease. Some were put to death.

Pirates in prison

Who is Long John Silver?

Long John Silver is a one-legged pirate. But he isn't real! He appears in a book called *Treasure Island*. This adventure story is all about pirates and buried treasure. It was written by Robert Louis Stevenson in 1883.

Long John Silver

What ate Captain Hook's hand?

Captain Hook is a fierce pirate in a story called *Peter Pan*. It was written as a book and a play by J.M. Barrie in 1904. Peter Pan is the hero. He cut off Captain Hook's hand and fed it to a crocodile. That's why the Captain needed a hook.

Captain Hook

Did pirates sing?

Gilbert and Sullivan were famous songwriters. They wrote a musical about pirates in 1879, called *Pirates of Penzance*. But the pirates were softies! They wouldn't steal from orphans – children who had no parents – so everyone pretended to be an orphan!

Write

Write your own pirate story. Your pirates can be kind or cruel. They could be modern pirates. What would treasure be like today?

Quiz time

Do you remember what you have read about pirates? These questions will test your memory. The pictures will help you. If you get stuck, read the pages again.

1. What is a pirate?

page 4

2. Who was afraid of the Barbarossas?

page 5

page 9

3. Who were the buccaneers?

4. Did sailors fight the pirates?

page 10

5. What did pirates do with their money?

page 10

6. Did pirates move about?

page 12

7. Whose prisoners ate caterpillars?

page 15

11. Where were all the jewels?

page 21

8. Where did pirates sleep?

page 16

12. Was the captain safe?

page 23

9. What did pirates eat?

page 17

13. What ate Captain Hook's hand?

page 29

page 18

10. Who was afraid of a flag?

Index